JUST FOR TODAY

101 Daily Reiki Meditations

by
Christopher W. Pritchard
&
Haley B. Steinhardt

Soul Tree Publications
www.SoulTreePublications.com
Cleveland, Ohio

First trade softcover edition 2019
Copyright © 2019 by Christopher W. Pritchard and Haley B. Steinhardt

All rights reserved. No part of this book may be reproduced, scanned, or distributed in any printed or electronic form without the explicit permission of the authors or publisher.

Publisher's Cataloging-in-Publication Data
Names: Pritchard, Christopher W., author | Steinhardt, Haley B., author.
Title: Just for Today: 101 Daily Reiki Meditations / Christopher W. Pritchard and Haley B. Steinhardt.
Description: First trade hardcover original edition. | A Soul Tree Publications book. | Cleveland, OH : Soul Tree Publications, 2019. | Includes index.
Identifiers: Library of Congress Control Number: 2019910033 | ISBN 978-1-733336-50-5
1. Reiki (Healing system). 2. Alternative medicine. 3. Integrative medicine.

The publisher and authors are not offering professional advice or services to the reader. No content herein is intended as a substitute fir consulting with a physician. Consult with a medical professional for any and all health-related matters. The publisher and authors shall not be liable or responsible for any loss or damage allegedly arising from any information or suggestions in this book.

www.SoulTreePublications.com

Table of Contents

Introduction	1
Kyo dake wa | Just for today	1
Shinpai sun a | Do not worry	2
Kansha shite | Be grateful	3
Gyo wo hage me | Work diligently	4
Hito ni shinsetsu ni | Be kind to myself and others	4
About This Workbook	5
Just for today…	
I am at peace.	6
I remember to smile.	8
I practice kindness.	10
I am grateful.	12
I practice self-love.	14
I forgive myself.	16
I forgive those who have hurt me.	18
I choose health.	20
I bless my food and drink.	22
I offer Reiki to a friend in need.	24
I send Reiki to my past.	26
I send Reiki to this present moment.	28
I send Reiki to my future.	30
I allow myself to trust.	32
I send Reiki to future generations.	34
I send Reiki to all who are hurting.	36
I send Reiki to those experiencing wartime.	38
I send Reiki for peace.	40
I send Reiki to healthcare workers.	42
I send Reiki to my work.	44
I send Reiki to my career path.	46
I send Reiki to local and national leaders.	48
I send Reiki to the sky.	50
I send Reiki to Mother Earth.	52
I send Reiki to my ancestors.	54
I send Reiki to my ego.	56
I send Reiki to children.	58
I send Reiki to elders.	60
I send Reiki to those giving birth.	62
I send Reiki to those who are dying.	64
I send Reiki to my home.	66
I send Reiki to my family.	68
I send Reiki to a concerning world event.	70
I send Reiki to my finances.	72
I send Reiki to the vehicles I travel in.	74
I send Reiki to all the drivers around me on the road.	76

I send Reiki to my highest purpose.	78
I send Reiki to my community.	80
I send Reiki to teachers.	82
I send Reiki to heal my fears.	84
I send Reiki to heal my wounds, illnesses, and injuries.	86
I send Reiki to my spiritual guides.	88
I speak only the truth.	90
I send Reiki to my dreams.	92
I send Reiki to a challenging relationship.	94
I send Reiki to my country.	96
I send Reiki to healing a bad habit.	98
I send Reiki to trees.	100
I send Reiki to animals.	102
I send Reiki to bees.	104
I send Reiki to my creativity.	106
I send Reiki to fathers.	108
I send Reiki to mothers.	110
I send Reiki to the day of my birth.	112
I send Reiki to a difficult choice.	114
I send Reiki to water.	116
I send Reiki to the air.	118
I send Reiki to those who are ill.	120
I send Reiki to the rainforest.	122
I send Reiki to heal global warming.	124
I honor my connection to all living things.	126
I accept help from others.	128
I acknowledge my own worth.	130
I allow myself to change and grow.	132
I celebrate my senses.	134
I honor the value of taking "little steps."	136
I remember that I am spirit.	138
I am optimistic and life affirming.	140
I freely and fearlessly express love.	142
I remain grounded and fully present in my life.	144
I accept all my emotions as valid.	146
I take the time to rest.	148
I choose to think less and "be" more.	150
I give myself Reiki.	152
I honor my Reiki family tree.	154
I share Reiki generously.	156
I am of service to others.	158
I am inspired.	160
I am productive.	162
I send Reiki to those who have lost a loved one.	164
I send Reiki to the worldwide Reiki community.	166
I send Reiki to my mental health.	168

I send Reiki to my spiritual health.	170
I send Reiki to setting healthy boundaries.	172
I send Reiki to those who have crossed over.	174
I send Reiki to artistic expression.	176
I send Reiki to those who serve.	178
I send Reiki to my sleep.	180
I send Reiki to those who are hungry.	182
I send Reiki to the homeless.	184
I send Reiki to the unemployed.	186
I send Reiki to my intuitive awareness.	188
I move with Reiki.	190
I send Reiki to my relationships.	192
I become a clearer channel for Reiki.	194
I send Reiki to a difficult moment in my past.	196
I send Reiki to my next step.	198
I send Reiki to science.	200
I send Reiki to plenty.	202
I remember that it can be easy.	204
I send Reiki to beginnings and endings.	206
Index	208

Introduction

As teachers and practitioners of Reiki, we offer these 101 "Just for Today" meditations with hope that they will encourage you to practice Reiki as a daily discipline – one that encourages an ever increasing measure of health, happiness, and love in your life.

We believe that Reiki is to be lived and experienced moment by moment. As we move beyond the study of Reiki towards an embodiment of Reiki, we begin to develop, perfect, and sustain a profound sense of personal growth. Day by day, our lives become more and more aligned with the life-affirming vibrations of universal Love.

Mikao Usui Sensei offered us the Gokai (Five Reiki Principles) believing them to be "the secret method for inviting blessings, the spiritual medicine of many illnesses." In Japanese the Gokai is as follows:

Kyo dake wa
Ikaru na
Shinpai su na
Kansha shite
Gyo wo hage me
Hito ni shinsetsu ni

While there are slight variations of the Gokai as they are translated from Japanese into other languages, we believe that each embodies the heart of Usui's original intention. For our part we believe that the Gokai expresses the following themes:

Kyo dake wa | Just for today

"Just for today" is the stated intention of living in the present moment. It is a choice we make to keep our focus on the here and now. This state of mindfulness is not tethered to a 24-hour clock, but rather to each breath and beat of our hearts. In the present moment, we proactively and thoughtfully choose our orientation to life. We choose where we place our focus of attention. We choose where and how to redirect our thoughts when they wander. We choose our words and actions. When we fail to live up to our best intentions, we can choose to reaffirm and simply begin again with the very next breath:

With this breath, I will not be angry.
With this beat of my heart I will choose to be calm and be loving.
I will immerse myself in the spirit of Reiki, right here and now, and intend that it will guide my thoughts, words, and deeds.

Ikaru na | Do not anger

Just for today, we can choose to avoid *choosing* anger. If and when anger arises, we can choose to release it, letting it wash over us like a wave. We can observe it without embracing or acting upon it. We can let it go without expression of malice or hurtful thoughts, words, or actions. If anger is simply one of the gears of this "vehicle" we drive through life, just for today we can choose to apply the brakes, shift into neutral, breathe, and calmly make a different choice:

I have not always avoided anger in the past; I will no doubt experience anger in the future. However, just for today – right here and now – I release all sense of annoyance and upset and I actively choose the gears of peace and calm and love.

Shinpai su na | Do not worry

We find principles of Reiki in alignment with those shared within the holy books of the world's religions. For example; just for today we need not worry.

- "There is no fear in love, but perfect love casts out fear." (1 John 4:18 ESV)

- "Do not worry; God is with us." (surah 9:40 Quran)

- "Why do you worry without cause?" (Bhagavad Gita)

- "If you have a problem that can be fixed, then there is no use in worrying. If you have a problem that cannot be fixed, then there is no use in worrying." (Buddhist proverb)

While worry and fear are genetically hardwired into the fight or flight mechanisms that helped humans evolve and survive, they are generally unproductive (in non-life-threatening situations) toward maintaining happy, healthy and productive lives. Fear-triggered adrenalin surges helped cavemen run from the sabretooth tiger, but when adrenalin is routinely released by worry and stress despite there being no imminent danger, it can cause a variety of harmful effects on our bodies such as insomnia, anxiety, rapid heartbeat, high blood pressure, and more.

Nonetheless, in our modern world it seems difficult to avoid stressors that may trigger worry and fear. From climate change to the latest shooting incident, from financial challenges to poor health, from partisan political warfare to literal warfare across our world, each day seems replete with open invitation to worry. The stated intention that *just for today I will not worry* frames our response as a matter of choice rather than animal instinct.

Any of us can easily choose to be fearful and to worry in this moment; many of us are well-practiced at such a response. Reiki encourages and empowers us to be more intentional less reactive:

Just for today, I will remember to breathe, meditate, and redirect the focus of my attention.
I can deliberately take meaningful and positive action to improve situations when possible. I can choose to peacefully and gracefully accept my human limitations when I cannot.

As stated above, in either case, there is no use in worrying. We believe Reiki embodies perfect love, and that perfect love casts out fear. Just for today, therefore, we can intend to exist mindfully, peacefully, and calmly amidst the storm. Do not worry; Love is with us.

Kansha shite | Be grateful

When reflecting upon Usui's assertion that the Gokai are "the secret method for inviting blessings, the spiritual medicine of many illnesses," consider that a grateful heart may be the cornerstone. When we remember all that we are thankful for in life, our heart naturally feels lighter, our mind grows increasingly calm, and our general disposition and outlook becomes brighter. We are more receptive to welcome life on its own terms right here and now without apprehension and fear. We become more trusting, open, and ready to give more generously to others. Moments of pain, suffering, worry, heartache, or stress may temporarily demand our attention yet quietly, in a reservoir of gratitude, is the elixir that will help us heal.

Pain distorts perception. The very moment of experiencing a sharp and piercing physical, emotional, or spiritual pain tends to hijack our senses. Laser focus on the sensation is also part of our physiological heritage. When we attend immediately and with great focus on the cause of pain, we may take action to escape it. When we remember the pain, we hope to prevent reoccurrence and further damage. We record tangential circumstances and players so as to trigger heightened vigilance in similar circumstances. Once we have touched the hot stove, we are less likely to touch it again.

The trouble with this survival mechanism is that it can permeate and compromise our mindful (here and now) approach to a happy and healthy life. If we remember only the pain of lost love, for example, we may be less likely to freely love again. If we take other risks in business, art, sport, or life and fail miserably and painfully, we may be inclined to risk less, live less spontaneously, and avoid new adventures and life experiences in the future. We may, therefore, miss much that could have enriched our life.

On the other hand, when just for today we choose gratitude, we remember all the good things we have been blessed with. We remember how fully alive we have been at times and can be again. Every painful relationship had some moments to be thankful for, some redeeming qualities that helped us grow and learn and experience and evolve to who we are today – and who we may yet become. Being grateful for the blessings we have had in the past and those we have now invites new blessings into our lives. We are more open and receptive and inviting when we are grateful. Gratitude triggers happiness and a peaceful feeling that – just right here and now – we are safe and life is good.

Just for today, I am grateful for all that I have learned through my many experiences.
Just for today, I am grateful for all the many blessings in my life, past and present.
Just for today, I allow gratitude to open my heart to new blessings coming my way.

Gyo wo hage me | Work diligently

Part of our purpose in life as human beings is to be the very best selves we can be: loving, peaceful, healthy, giving, and productive. Our lives matter, and we can use them to make a difference in the world – just for today. (We aren't merely here to take up space and resources and then die! Our work is to contribute to the ever-unfolding story of humanity and life.

Just for today, I dedicate my work to enrich not only the quality of my own life, but also the lives of my loved ones, my community, and the world.
Just for today I focus my intention on my contribution to existence – to a faithful attention towards purposeful living.
Just for today, I choose to work diligently, to discover and evolve toward my highest and best self.

Hito ni shinsetsu ni | Be kind to myself and others

We are sometimes our own worst critic, so it's no surprise how easy it can be to criticize others. At times, we disappoint ourselves and think or act unkindly toward ourselves. At times, we think or act unkindly to others. Moreover, we often neglect to embody the intentional practice of everyday kindness – common courtesy and positive regard toward one another. What many don't realize is that kindness is a means to improving our own health and happiness in addition to that of those around us.

Just for today I will proactively and intentionally be kind.
I will give myself and others the benefit of the doubt.
I will be slow to anger, quick to praise, and display goodwill toward all whom I encounter.

To be present and mindful with the explicitly stated goal of manifesting kindness is a daily practice that yields blessings and health to all within its light.

About This Workbook

This workbook is designed to engage you not only in reading but in daily action and reflection. We hope and believe it will encourage you to bring the Gokai to life through daily intention setting, mindful execution, and reflection. We trust that taking time to jot down your personal thoughts on how the daily intention impacted your day and your life in the NOTE section after each "Just for Today" meditation will also yield increased blessings and the health-affirming outcomes that Mikao Usui envisioned.

We are so grateful you have chosen to join us on this Reiki journey… just for today.

Namaste,

Chris Pritchard & Haley Steinhardt

1.

Just for today...

I am at peace.

Just for today, I am at peace. I allow myself to have a calm and peaceful heart. When I encounter upsetting thoughts or feelings, I take a deep, calming breath, close my eyes, and say the words, "I am at peace." I take time to meditate by gently closing my eyes, inhaling deeply, and speaking the words "I am at peace" with each exhale in a mantra-like fashion. Just for today, I send Reiki to calm my body, mind, and spirit and infuse my whole self with love, light, and peaceful energy.

My "Just for Today" Journal Entry

2.

Just for today...

I remember to smile.

Just for today, I remember to smile. I smile at myself in the mirror. I smile to myself when I am alone. I smile at the people I see, whether or not I know them. I smile at the earth and the sun and the moon and the natural world around me. I send Reiki to my heart as I take slow, deep breaths and keep smiling. I radiate this smile inward through every cell of my being. I radiate this smile outward to shine love and light and positivity on all I encounter today.

My "Just for Today" Journal Entry

3.

Just for today...

I practice kindness.

Just for today, I practice kindness. I think kind thoughts and speak kind words to myself and others. I focus on kindness in every interaction I have with the people I encounter. I intend that Reiki align my mind, heart, and spirit with love and goodwill towards others. I pay attention and stay present in each moment to find simple ways I may show kindness. I hold open a door for a stranger, rake a neighbor's leaves, send a note of encouragement to a friend who is going through a difficult time, or cook a special dinner for my family. I put my heart of kindness into action, and I do so without need for recognition or validation from others. I practice kindness for kindness' sake.

My "Just for Today" Journal Entry

4.

Just for today…

I am grateful.

Just for today, I am grateful. I have gratitude for the food I eat, the shelter over my head, and the air that I breathe. I am grateful for the many life lessons that have brought me to this moment. I am grateful for each joy I have experienced and grateful I have survived each hardship I have encountered. I am grateful to be here now, filled with gratitude for the many blessings in my life. I make a list of all the things I am grateful for, big and small, taking the time to write down anything that comes to mind. I intend that Reiki helps me to remember all the love and blessings in my life so that my heart may be filled to overflowing with a deep sense of gratitude.

My "Just for Today" Journal Entry

5.

Just for today…

I practice self-love.

Just for today, I practice self-love. I allow love to flow to my whole self—my body, my mind, and my spirit. I offer love to the parts of myself that I like and the parts I wish were different. I send love to the parts of me I can change and the parts I can't. Just for today, I invite Reiki to flow through me and remind me that I am loved and I am worthy of love. I practice looking at myself in the mirror, deeply looking into my own eyes and saying, "I love you." I remember that it's okay if this feels awkward at first or if I have trouble believing this. I know that Reiki honors intention and that, in time, I will learn to love myself more completely. I send Reiki to my heart and to my whole being, filling myself up with love and light.

My "Just for Today" Journal Entry

6.

Just for today…

I forgive myself.

Just for today, I forgive myself. I acknowledge all the things I have done that I believe were wrong. I acknowledge everything I have done that has hurt me or hurt others, whether knowingly or unknowingly. I allow myself to feel sorry for participating in these hurtful thoughts, words, and actions. Just for today, I send Reiki to myself with the intention of forgiveness. Just for today, I forgive myself completely, allowing Reiki to fill me with love and peace and a deep sense of forgiveness. I allow forgiveness to wash over me and give me a fresh start.

My "Just for Today" Journal Entry

7.

Just for today...

I forgive those who have hurt me.

Just for today, I forgive those who have hurt me. I call to mind anyone who has ever been the source of my pain or suffering and I offer each of them forgiveness. In doing so, I know that forgiveness does not mean I condone their hurtful actions. Instead, I acknowledge that forgiveness means I release myself from the burden of taking on any further hurt from these past wrongs. I also acknowledge that for those in my life who may continue to hurt me, I can forgive them in this moment to help myself heal and support myself in disengaging from their hurtful behavior. I send Reiki to myself with the intention that it foster and sustain a true spirit of forgiveness within me. I send Reiki across time and space to facilitate the Reiki of forgiveness reaching the people, places, and situations that are willing and able to accept it. Just for today I meditate on forgiveness, knowing that as I forgive, I heal.

My "Just for Today" Journal Entry

8.

Just for today…

I choose health.

Just for today, I choose health. I honor this physical temple with love and gratitude. I send Reiki to myself with the intention that it helps me remain conscious and purposeful with regard to the food and drink I allow to enter my body. I give my body all it needs to function healthfully. I allow fresh water and fresh, whole foods to flush toxins from my body. I move my body consciously to give it the daily exercise it needs. I am mindful of the thoughts I have about my body and my health, allowing unhelpful thoughts to drift past me and focusing instead on positive, healthy ones. I honor this body that serves as the sacred vessel for my soul with respect and compassion. I send Reiki to my highest purpose, intending that it supports me in aligning my thoughts and actions with my optimal health and well-being.

My "Just for Today" Journal Entry

9.

Just for today...

I bless my food and drink.

Just for today, I bless my food and drink. Each time I sit down to invite food or drink into my body, I pause to give thanks to all the people who helped grow, prepare, and deliver my food. I send Reiki blessings to them and their families. I offer gratitude to the plant or animal beings who gave of their bodies so I could nourish my body. I honor them and send blessings to their life essence. I send Reiki to human laws, intending that they continue to move towards respect and kind treatment of all beings, including those who are part of the food system. I allow Reiki to flow into my food and drink, intending that all negativity be released and replaced with love and light. I eat and drink knowing that my food nourishes my whole self and blesses all who have touched it.

My "Just for Today" Journal Entry

10.

Just for today...

I offer Reiki to a friend in need.

Just for today, I offer Reiki to a friend in need. I open myself to be a clear channel for Reiki healing and I allow Reiki to flow through me, intending that it support this person and go to their highest good. I know that Reiki is not bound by time or space and can reach this person anywhere in the universe as well as in the past, present, or future. I offer Reiki knowing that it will only reach this individual if and when they are open to receiving it, which may or may not be right now. I trust that the Reiki energy meant for them will reach them exactly when they need it most.

My "Just for Today" Journal Entry

11.

Just for today…

I send Reiki to my past.

Just for today, I send Reiki to my past. I ask my ego to step back so I may become a clear channel for Reiki energy and I allow Reiki to flow through me and into my past, strengthening me in the times I felt weakest, supporting me through my most difficult moments, healing my deepest wounds. I gratefully welcome that healing as it ripples through time and space from the past into this moment, creating a stronger, more supported, and healthier present version of myself.

My "Just for Today" Journal Entry

12.

Just for today...

I send Reiki to this present moment.

Just for today, I send Reiki to this present moment. I allow Reiki to fill up my body, mind, spirit, and all my surroundings. I invite Reiki to cleanse and clear all negativity I may be carrying, or which may be held by any person, place, or object in my vicinity. Reiki flows freely and is readily available to all around me who are willing to receive it. Reiki flows from me through my body and my surroundings on outward into my community and beyond, flowing over every part of the Earth, offering a moment of peace and healing to any and all who are open to it. Reiki flows outward into the universe, filling every particle of existence completely. I feel a deep sense of peace within as I experience Reiki permeating all aspects of this present moment.

My "Just for Today" Journal Entry

13.

Just for today...

I send Reiki to my future.

Just for today, I send Reiki to my future. Without being attached to a specific outcome, I send Reiki to future events in my life with the intention that they unfold in a way that supports my highest purpose, joy, and well-being. I allow Reiki to flow through me to my future path, across time and space, knowing that Reiki supports me in creating the clearest, gentlest way forward to living my happiest, most-fulfilling life. I intend that Reiki eases my passage through the challenges ahead so that I learn my life lessons as gently as possible and achieve my highest purpose. I let go of any worry about my future, trusting the light and love of the universe to take care of me.

My "Just for Today" Journal Entry

14.

Just for today ...

I allow myself to trust.

Just for today, I allow myself to trust. I send Reiki to myself with the intention that it fosters a trusting spirit in me. I allow Reiki to flow through me to any part of me that is resistant to trusting and I allow Reiki to heal it. I let go of the need to control life. I let go of the illusion that life is controllable. I allow myself to trust in divine timing, even though I may not understand it. I trust that things are falling into place in just the right way to help me fulfill my highest purpose, even if some of the pieces are challenging for me. I let go of fear and worry. As I let go and trust, I am at peace.

My "Just for Today" Journal Entry

15.

Just for today...

I send Reiki to future generations.

Just for today, I send Reiki to future generations. I allow Reiki healing and blessings to flow through me to those yet to be born. Let Reiki bless the births and lives of those who are the future caretakers of our planet. Let Reiki support them in learning their life lessons with ease in a community filled with love. May their lives be blessed with joy, companionship, and purpose. Let Reiki ease their eventual passing, blessing all who have known them, and blessing the generations to follow. I have gratitude in my heart, knowing that love and light are filling the generations to come and creating a more peaceful, joyful existence for all.

My "Just for Today" Journal Entry

16.

Just for today...

I send Reiki to all who are hurting.

Just for today, I send Reiki to all who are hurting. Knowing that Reiki never forces, I become a clear channel for Reiki so that healing light may flow through me and be received by all who wish to receive it at exactly the time they need it most. Let Reiki flow to ease their suffering. Let Reiki guide and support them toward healing and renewal. Let Reiki move them beyond pain toward wellness of body, mind, and spirit so they may experience their highest purpose. May Reiki blessings be available to all who are suffering.

My "Just for Today" Journal Entry

17.

Just for today...

I send Reiki to those experiencing wartime.

Just for today, I send Reiki to those experiencing wartime. Reiki flows to heal the cause of war and toward resolution, peace, balance, and compassion. Let light and love protect and comfort those who find themselves in wartime through no choice of their own. Let healing light and love flows to those who choose to participate in wartime. Reiki blessings flow through me to all beings to support them in healing completely and being free from war.

My "Just for Today" Journal Entry

18.

Just for today...

I send Reiki for peace.

Just for today, I send Reiki for peace. May all beings be free from suffering and experience peace, both within themselves and in the physical world around them. May Reiki bless all beings with peacefulness. May the light and love of the universe penetrate even the darkest places within, just as water softens stone and finds its way into even the smallest cracks. Just for today, may all of existence be in harmony with itself. May Reiki energy resolve confusion, conflict, and war. May Reiki guide all who are willing to receive it towards peace of body, mind, and spirit.

My "Just for Today" Journal Entry

19.

Just for today...

I send Reiki to healthcare workers.

Just for today, I send Reiki to healthcare workers. I honor those who give of themselves in service to others who are hurting, ill, or incapacitated. May Reiki support them in staying in touch with their compassion. May it give them strength, perseverance, and energy to navigate the most challenging moments. May Reiki flow to heal and protect their bodies, minds, and spirits as they provide for so many. May those in their care experience the joy of connection and be blessed with the energy of gratitude. Reiki flows through me to clear the spaces they work within of all negativity, facilitating healing for all.

My "Just for Today" Journal Entry

20.

Just for today...

I send Reiki to my work.

Just for today, I send Reiki to my work. May Reiki bless my hands and my feet, my heart and my brain so I may work diligently, joyfully, and creatively to complete my projects. I allow Reiki to guide me in producing my best work and in attracting work into my life that is alignment with my highest purpose. I honor the role of work in my life as a teacher. Reiki flows to support healthy communications with others as I complete my work. I feel calm, clear, and focused as I work with ease and joy.

My "Just for Today" Journal Entry

21.

Just for today...

I send Reiki to my career path.

Just for today, I send Reiki to my career path. Reiki flows to my current career situation, blessing it with love and light and working to unfold a path ahead towards my highest good. Reiki blesses the work I do and all who work with me. Reiki clears the way for me to achieve my personal best in my career. Reiki flows to support me in affecting my family, friends, and community positively through the work I do. Reiki continuously supports me in finding and maintaining the career path that is best for my personal growth, happiness, and financial stability.

My "Just for Today" Journal Entry

22.

Just for today...

I send Reiki to local and national leaders.

Just for today, I send Reiki to local and national leaders. Reiki flows through me to leaders all over the world, supporting them in becoming aware of their continual access to love and light, encouraging compassionate action in their roles as caretakers for their communities and countries. Reiki flows to reveal the path that is of the highest good for all the people of Earth to each and every leader. Reiki supports all those in leadership in having all they need to achieve peace and well-being for the people they serve.

My "Just for Today" Journal Entry

23.

Just for today...

I send Reiki to the sky.

Just for today, I send Reiki to the sky. I invite mindfulness throughout this day of the beauty and mysteries of the universe. I am grateful for the life-sustaining power of the sun. I honor the cycles of the moon and the pull it has on the water in my body and the waters of our planet. I look at the night sky and am reminded that I am made of stardust. I honor the clouds and their ever-changing beauty. I send Reiki of gratitude for the rain that cleanses and feeds our world. With a joyful heart, I allow Reiki to flow through as I am filled with appreciation for the magnificence of planet Earth's skies.

My "Just for Today" Journal Entry

24.

Just for today...

I send Reiki to Mother Earth.

Just for today, I send Reiki to Mother Earth. I remember that the planet beneath my feet contains the very ingredients that make up my physical body, the clothes on my back, the roof over my head, and the food on my table. I am grateful for the rich and vibrant tapestry of life Earth sustains—two-leggeds, four-leggeds, winged ones, finned ones, insects, trees, oceans and rivers, stones and mountains. Earth contains so many sacred earth energies, and I honor them with Reiki today. I open myself to be a clear channel for Reiki energy to flow to all the beings and energies of Earth, blessing and healing them as, like a tree, I remember to stay grounded so I may walk in balance even as I reach for greater spiritual awareness.

My "Just for Today" Journal Entry

25.

Just for today...

I send Reiki to my ancestors.

Just for today, I send Reiki to my ancestors. I allow Reiki to flow through me, traversing time and space to reach all those who have come before and made it possible for me to be here, now, in this body learning these lessons. I offer healing and gratitude to each of them, known or unknown, trusting that Reiki touches each of their lives and beings in the way that is meant for them. I honor my DNA and this physical temple that is my body, knowing that I would not reside in it without those who have come before.

My "Just for Today" Journal Entry

26.

Just for today...

I send Reiki to my ego.

Just for today, I send Reiki to my ego. Reiki flows to my ego, giving it all the support it needs to be able and willing to step aside completely during my Reiki practice. I intend that Reiki fills me with a deep sense of peace, calm, and safety. I allow Reiki to give me the confidence I need to step aside, as a threatened ego finds this too difficult. Reiki flows to strengthen and support my ego in being a healthy, balanced part of my human experience so I may make ever healthier, kinder, and more compassionate choices. Just for today, I invite my ego to make way for me to be a clear channel for the love and light of Reiki to shine through me with optimal strength and purity towards fostering and supporting my highest purpose and that of all whom I encounter.

My "Just for Today" Journal Entry

27.

Just for today...

I send Reiki to children.

Just for today, I send Reiki to children. Reiki blessings flow to all the children of the world, supporting them in learning their lessons gently and easily as they navigate their paths to their highest good. Reiki flows to their hearts, blessing and healing them. Reiki flows to their bodies, supporting them in healthy functioning. Reiki flows to their education, supporting them in learning all they need to know to walk in kindness and compassion in the world. Reiki flows to their families, blessing their homes, blessing their communications, blessing their way to joyful abundance. Reiki flows to protect and bless all children, everywhere.

My "Just for Today" Journal Entry

28.

Just for today...

I send Reiki to elders.

Just for today, I send Reiki to elders. Reiki flows to all the elders of the world, blessing them with the energy of gratitude for their life experience and their teachings, blessing their physical bodies to be comfortable and cared for, blessing their emotional and spiritual bodies to be clear in their reflections on this earth walk. I honor all of our elders, knowing that each and every one of them has made—and continues to make—an impact on this world. I am grateful to have been given an opportunity to learn from their words and actions.

My "Just for Today" Journal Entry

29.

Just for today...

I send Reiki to those giving birth.

Just for today, I send Reiki to those giving birth. Reiki blessings of joy and gentleness flow to all mothers and babies experiencing birth, human and animal alike. Reiki blesses the birth experience for all who are part of it, allowing deep healing and powerful life lessons to emerge during and after. Reiki flows to support a safe and smooth transition for mothers and babies as life passes from the womb into the world. I honor all who give birth, and send Reiki for protection and health for mothers and babies during and after the birthing process.

My "Just for Today" Journal Entry

30.

Just for today...

I send Reiki to those who are dying.

Just for today, I send Reiki to those who are dying. May Reiki bless your transition with peace and gentleness. May you have comfort and find resolution within your heart for any lingering troubles from this life. May you know that your journey does not end here, and that you are loved eternally with an unwavering, pure love that is vaster and deeper than anything else in existence. May you be carried from your mortal body in peace and cradled by your guardians as you expand into the spiritual realm.

My "Just for Today" Journal Entry

31.

Just for today...

I send Reiki to my home.

Just for today, I send Reiki to my home. Starting in the East, I bless the entire East side of my home with Reiki, cleansing and clearing all negativity and unhelpful energy and replacing it with love and light. Then I turn to the South, blessing the entire South side of my home with Reiki, cleansing and clearing it completely, filling it up with love and light. Then I do the West side; next the North; then I bless the areas of my home above below me. I bless all the spaces in between that flow through my home. Finally, I bless the land that holds my home and the sky above it, offering gratitude and cleansing and clearing it. I bless all the beings who live in my home and on the land around my home with joy and gentleness and all the support they need to achieve their highest purpose. Reiki flows to ensure that all who come to my home enter peacefully, and Reiki blesses their time here.

My "Just for Today" Journal Entry

32.

Just for today…

I send Reiki to my family.

Just for today, I send Reiki to my family. Knowing that Reiki never forces, I offer Reiki to be received by any member of my family who is willing to receive it, including myself. May Reiki heal the parts of each of us that we are willing to heal, and may it support us in becoming ready to heal any areas we may not yet be open to working on. Reiki flows through me to bless our lives, individually and together, with joy and gentleness. May we learn our lessons with ease so that we become ever more at peace with ourselves and each other. May our hearts, minds, words, and actions be filled with love and compassion. May we gently heal and grow.

My "Just for Today" Journal Entry

33.

Just for today...

I send Reiki to a concerning world event.

Just for today, I send Reiki to a concerning world event. I see Reiki healing energy flowing to ease the suffering of all involved. I send Reiki for protection of all who are at risk. Reiki flows to bring peace and healing to all. I ask that Reiki give courage and wisdom to first responders and all who come to the aid of others. I ask that Reiki guide outcomes and restoration of body, mind, and spirit to let goodness and love and light shine amidst even the most difficult circumstances so the highest purpose of all impacted may yet be realized. Just for today, I allow myself to be a clear channel for Reiki energy so that it may reach the source of the issue and heal it. Reiki flows to protect all beings from further harm, and to support a peaceful and compassionate resolution.

My "Just for Today" Journal Entry

34.

Just for today...

I send Reiki to my finances.

Just for today, I send Reiki to my finances. Reiki flows to support me in experiencing joyful abundance. I allow myself to let go of any thoughts, ideas, or other obstacles that may have kept me from experiencing financial abundance in my life. I send Reiki to my own inner peacefulness around my finances, and to knowing and being grateful for having all that I need. Reiki supports me in letting go of all worry and stress. As a clear channel for Reiki, I know that joyful abundance and healthy prosperity flow freely to me, and I trust in the universal life force energy to provide all that I need for my physical, emotional, mental, spiritual, and financial well-being.

My "Just for Today" Journal Entry

35.

Just for today...

I send Reiki to the vehicles I travel in.

Just for today, I send Reiki to the vehicles I travel in. Reiki flows to surround the vehicles that carry me with white light, cradling them in safety and protecting all passengers within. Reiki flows to the mechanical parts, blessing them to work perfectly to protect all within and around each vehicle I use, blessing them with malfunction only when it will protect me and others from harm. I trust in the divine timing of events like traffic jams, detours and delays, lost keys, and broken down vehicles, knowing that Reiki supports me and protects me in many ways, even unexpected ones that I may not recognize or understand as they are happening. Reiki protects and guides me in all aspects of my physical and spiritual journey.

My "Just for Today" Journal Entry

36.

Just for today...

I send Reiki to all the drivers around me on the road.

Just for today, I send Reiki to all the drivers around me on the road. Knowing that Reiki never forces, I allow myself to become a clear channel for Reiki to flow to all drivers as fellow travelers on this road with me. Let Reiki protect each of them and their passengers, carrying them safely to their destinations. Reiki flows to ease any road stress and replace it with calm, clear, compassionate thoughts. Reiki supports me in remaining calm, clear, and compassionate even when I encounter angry drivers. Reiki flows between all our vehicles, protecting us and supporting us in traveling safely and calmly.

My "Just for Today" Journal Entry

37.

Just for today...

I send Reiki to my highest purpose.

Just for today, I send Reiki to my highest purpose. Reiki flows through me with ease as I set my ego aside and become a clear channel for the love and light of this universal life force energy. My highest purpose and best next steps come to my awareness at just the right moment each and every day of my life. Reiki supports me in overcoming challenges with ease and grace so that I may learn my lessons at the perfect time to blossom into my fullest potential. Reiki flows through me with each step I take, guiding me and supporting me in discovering my path and staying the course through all of life's ups and downs.

My "Just for Today" Journal Entry

38.

Just for today...

I send Reiki to my community.

Just for today, I send Reiki to my community. Reiki blesses the health and safety of my community. Reiki flows to the educational system and the local government. Reiki shines into the hearts of each and every member of my community, blessing them with all they need to thrive. Reiki flows to the land that holds my community, and to all beings within and upon it. I send Reiki with the intention that this community be a safe haven for all who live and visit here. I intend that Reiki encourage optimal stewardship of our air and water and natural resources. I send Reiki to the businesses that serve this community. I ask that Reiki guide them in the provision of products and services to the enrichment of all they serve. Let Reiki bring love and peace and goodwill to this community that transcends religious, political, and racial lines that might otherwise divide us. Let Reiki shine across and throughout this community, that it may be a welcoming and inspiring beacon to all who see it.

My "Just for Today" Journal Entry

39.

Just for today...

I send Reiki to teachers.

Just for today, I send Reiki to teachers. Reiki flows to all of my own teachers, past, present, and future so they may receive it exactly when they need it most. Reiki flows to the teachers of others, to all teachers worldwide. I offer Reiki blessings so that all teachers may have an abundance of the support and resources they need to do their good work. Reiki blessings flow to their communication so it may be clear and compassionate and reach their students with ease, giving them all they need to thrive in this world. May all teachers be appreciated and celebrated by their communities. Reiki flows, too, to honor the truth that all we encounter is our teacher. Let us honor the teacher within each other and within our experiences, even when the lessons are difficult. Reiki flows to support us in all teaching and learning.

My "Just for Today" Journal Entry

40.

Just for today...

I send Reiki to heal my fears.

Just for today, I send Reiki to heal my fears. Let Reiki illuminate the truth within me that love heals fear. Let Reiki guide my body, mind, and spirit gently yet unequivocally away from fearful thoughts. Let Reiki align my energies with love and light so as to reveal the illusionary nature of fear. In this way, I can see fear as external to me, like a powerless vapor or mist that evaporates in the bright sunshine and I am healed of the illusion of its power over me. When I feel fear, I focus my attention on the flow of Reiki into my mind, body, and spirit. Reiki heals the place within me that housed the fear. Reiki replaces any remaining fear within me with love and light, filling me up with trust and love, flowing steadily and continuously to heal me.

My "Just for Today" Journal Entry

41.

Just for today...

I send Reiki to heal my wounds, illnesses, and injuries.

Just for today, I send Reiki to heal my wounds, illnesses, and injuries, whether past or present. I allow Reiki to flow freely through my body and through time and space, finding those places that need healing whether they be in the past, present, or future. Reiki goes straight to the root cause of the injury or illness and provides gentle healing energy. Reiki travels to the moment injury or illness first occurred and softens it, lessening its impact and rippling out healing energy so I may feel healthy and whole in each moment. Reiki flows to heal me completely, removing all the roots and layers of my injury or illness.

My "Just for Today" Journal Entry

42.

Just for today...

I send Reiki to my spiritual guides.

Just for today, I send Reiki to my spiritual guides. Reiki guides and protects me, connecting me with the spiritual guides who are meant for me, ensuring that I only hear and receive spiritual guidance that comes from pure love and light and is intended for my highest purpose. I offer Reiki and gratitude for all the help and guidance I have received, known and unknown. I open myself to be a clear channel for Reiki and call upon Reiki to bless all spiritual guides and guidance I receive to better align me with love. May Reiki bless my spiritual guides to receive my love and gratitude and may all our interactions be blessed eternally by the source of all love, light, and joy.

My "Just for Today" Journal Entry

43.

Just for today…

I speak only the truth.

Just for today, I speak only the truth. I commit to communicating truthfully in all my interactions, no matter how small, both virtually and in person. I take the time I need to choose words that express my truth clearly and kindly. I notice and correct myself if I find myself speaking "automatically" out of habit in a way that is not aligned with ultimate truthfulness. Reiki flows to support me in communicating truthfully with compassion and mindfulness. I feel empowered by my ability to speak, act, and live truthfully.

My "Just for Today" Journal Entry

44.

Just for today…

I send Reiki to my dreams.

Just for today, I send Reiki to my dreams. Reiki flows to my dreamtime, blessing me with greater awareness of my dreams and a greater ability to understand, remember, and process them. Reiki blesses my dreamtime as a sacred realm for me to receive spiritual information that can help me in my waking life. Reiki supports me in my dreaming visions, sending me the information I need to receive in the safe environment of dreams. Reiki flows through me strongly in the dreamtime, whether in good dreams or troubling ones. Reiki helps me to shift troubling dreams, giving me strength and confidence in my connection to Reiki.

My "Just for Today" Journal Entry

45.

Just for today...

I send Reiki to a challenging relationship.

Just for today, I send Reiki to a challenging relationship. Knowing that Reiki never forces, I offer Reiki to be made available to this person if and when they are willing to receive it, trusting that it will arrive to them at the time they need it most, whether or not that is right now. I shine a Reiki light on the places in my body where an unhealthy connection exists between me and this other person. Reiki flows to this energy cord, along with its entire root system, removing it completely from my body and dissolving it into love and light. Reiki takes care of this for the other person, as well, when they are ready to receive this healing energy. Reiki flows to our communication and interactions, filling them with love, light, and compassion. Reiki flows to allow forgiveness and loving kindness between us.

My "Just for Today" Journal Entry

46.

Just for today...

I send Reiki to my country.

Just for today, I send Reiki to my country. Reiki blesses and heals the land, air, and water of my country. Reiki flows to all the citizens and leaders who wish to accept it, filling their hearts with peace, joy, and compassion. For all those who are not now ready or willing to heal, Reiki blessings are not bound by time or space and exist to support any and all beings the moment they are ready to receive healing. Reiki blesses all the plants and animals and all other beings in my country, supporting them in having healthy habitats, being treated with respect, and receiving all they need to thrive in balance and harmony with one another and with our human family. Let Reiki guide my country's interaction with other countries. Let my country encourage peace over war, justice over injustice, plenty over want, and equality over inequality. Just for today, let Reiki bless the confluence of hearts, resources, circumstances, and intentions existing within my country, that it may be a beacon of love and light for those all over the world.

My "Just for Today" Journal Entry

47.

Just for today...

I send Reiki to healing a bad habit.

Just for today, I send Reiki to healing a bad habit. In recognizing I have a habit that feels very difficult for me to break, I ask for support and assistance in leaving it behind. I allow myself to be a clear channel for Reiki energy so that Reiki can penetrate the darkest corners of my resistance and heal the root of the issue. I invite Reiki to heal me completely, and I trust the source of all love and light to support me in removing this bad habit from my existence while healing the part of me that created it.

My "Just for Today" Journal Entry

48.

Just for today...

I send Reiki to trees.

Just for today, I send Reiki to trees. With each breath in, I send Reiki in thanks to the trees for providing me with oxygen to breathe. With each breath out, I send Reiki in thanks to the trees for their ability to transform the carbon dioxide I exhale into fresh air for me to breathe. I honor you, trees, in the way that you remind me to stay grounded even as I reach for new spiritual heights. I honor you for the wood you provide that allows us to have and use so many helpful things in our day-to-day lives, from paper, to tables and chairs, to our very homes, and more. I am grateful for the shade you provide in summer and the beautiful leaves in fall. I'm grateful for your strong silhouette against the snow and ice in winter, and you who remain evergreen year round. You remind me to bring quiet strength and courage to the cold, dark times in my own life. I am grateful for the buds that burst into existence with fresh, new energy from your outstretched branches in the spring. Just for today, I send Reiki blessings of gratitude and healthy growth to all the trees of our planet.

My "Just for Today" Journal Entry

49.

Just for today...

I send Reiki to animals.

Just for today, I send Reiki to animals. I offer Reiki to all the animals in my world—to pets and wildlife, to the birds, bugs, fish, mammals, and other creatures on the land around me. Reiki flows to heal any wounds or illness they may be experiencing. Reiki blesses them with enough food, water, and shelter to thrive in balance with one another. Reiki blesses all beings to be free from cruelty and suffering. I offer Reiki in gratitude for the companionship and happiness animals bring to so many, for the sacrifices made for the sustenance of other beings, and for the lessons learned as I observe animals in nature. May Reiki flow to bless all the animal life of planet Earth to fulfill its highest purpose with ease and grace.

My "Just for Today" Journal Entry

50.

Just for today...

I send Reiki to bees.

Just for today, I send Reiki to bees. I send Reiki and gratitude for the abundance of life sustained by the bees as they pollinate the flowers of our planet. As I enjoy flowers and fruits and the healthy life cycle of the animal kingdom around me, I send Reiki and give thanks for the bees in our world. Let Reiki flow to correct the laws and practices of humans that have threatened the bee population. Let Reiki support the alignment of our hearts, minds, and actions so that bee populations return to and remain in healthy abundance, existing in balance with all beings.

My "Just for Today" Journal Entry

51.

Just for today...

I send Reiki to my creativity.

Just for today, I send Reiki to my creativity. I allow Reiki to flow into my heart space and remove all blockages to my creativity, gently and completely. Reiki supports me in birthing creative ideas and manifesting completion on my creative projects. In send Reiki to bless my creative spirit today with the courage to convey my truth without fear and without hesitation or self-censorship. Reiki flows to help me become playful and spontaneous, joyful and productive, focused and purposeful. I express my creativity fully and freely from the heart and share it with the world.

My "Just for Today" Journal Entry

52.

Just for today...

I send Reiki to fathers.

Just for today, I send Reiki to fathers. Reiki flows to bless all those who serve as fathers to other beings. To all those fathers who wish to receive healing energy, Reiki flows into the deepest aspects of their being, filling them with healing love and light, transforming the most difficult struggles into manageable lessons. Reiki blesses all fathers and supports them in achieving their highest life's purpose.

My "Just for Today" Journal Entry

53.

Just for today…

I send Reiki to mothers.

Just for today, I send Reiki to mothers. Reiki flows to all who serve as mothers to other beings. To any mothers who are open to receiving healing energy, Reiki flows to their hearts and supports them in shining and healing and growing into their best selves. Reiki blesses them with all they need to care for themselves and others, flowing forward and backward in time to ease their life's journey.

My "Just for Today" Journal Entry

54.

Just for today...

I send Reiki to the day of my birth.

Just for today, I send Reiki to the day of my birth. Reiki blesses my passage into this world, allowing me to overcome any obstacles so I could grow and learn and be here, now. Reiki blesses all who were present at my birth, giving them the strength they needed in those moments, blessing their hearts with gentleness and joy. Reiki flows to every aspect of my birth and blesses it for the highest purpose of all who helped bring me into the world.

My "Just for Today" Journal Entry

55.

Just for today...

I send Reiki to a difficult choice.

Just for today, I send Reiki to a difficult choice. I allow my ego to step back so I may be a clear channel for Reiki energy to flow through me and support me in making the best choices for my highest good. I give myself the time I need to allow the best choice to become clear to me, trusting that Reiki flows to all involved to bless the outcome.

My "Just for Today" Journal Entry

56.

Just for today...

I send Reiki to water.

Just for today, I send Reiki to water. I honor the lifeblood of our planet that is water, allowing Reiki to flow through me to bless all water to be clean and clear. I honor the water that makes up more than half of my body, the water that rains down from the sky, the water that flows through rivers and streams and lakes and oceans all over the earth. In blessing and connecting with the water within me, I bless and connect with all water. Reiki flows to support all water in being healthy and whole, now and for all future generations.

My "Just for Today" Journal Entry

57.

Just for today...

I send Reiki to the air.

Just for today, I send Reiki to the air. Reiki blesses the sacred exchange of air that flows through our atmosphere, through our trees and plants, and through all the physical beings of our planet. Reiki supports the air in being clean and clear so all beings may breathe easily and enjoy good health. Reiki flows with ease and grace, in and out with my own breath, blessing my body and my health as it flows out to bless all the air of our planet.

My "Just for Today" Journal Entry

58.

Just for today...

I send Reiki to those who are ill.

Just for today, I send Reiki to those who are ill. Reiki flows with ease to all struggling with illness who are open to receiving healing. Healing light hones in on the source of the illness and heals its very roots, spreading healing out in gentle waves all through the body. Reiki supports all those who are ill in resolving the illness to the best outcome for their highest life's purpose. Reiki flows freely to transform all suffering into healing light.

My "Just for Today" Journal Entry

59.

Just for today...

I send Reiki to the rainforest.

Just for today, I send Reiki to the rainforest. Reiki flows to surround and fill the rainforest with love and light. Healing light flows into the hearts of all beings who have an influence on maintaining and recovering our rainforests, including those who have sought only to use it for their own purposes. Reiki energy flows to all beings who are open to receiving healing, allowing powerful shifts in consciousness to take place so that the highest purpose of our planet and our rainforests may be fulfilled. Reiki blesses all the creatures of the rainforests with love, light, and protection so they may thrive in their natural environment.

My "Just for Today" Journal Entry

60.

Just for today...

I send Reiki to heal global warming.

Just for today, I send Reiki to heal global warming. Reiki flows to support all beings in becoming more conscious of our impact on this planet we share. Reiki flows to support Mother Earth in healing herself, as is her nature when uninterrupted or uncompromised by human actions. Reiki supports the human population in shifting as a whole to be stewards of the Earth. Reiki blesses all efforts to walk in balance and make different choices to lessen human causes of global warming. Reiki flows to protect all beings from global warming, and to reverse its effects.

My "Just for Today" Journal Entry

61.

Just for today...

I honor my connection to all living things.

Just for today, I honor my connection to all living things. I acknowledge and offer gratitude to the universal life force energy that is Reiki, a unifying field of love and light that connects me with all living things. I recognize the simple truth that our sense of separateness is an illusion. I readily feel this connection when I sit quietly and observe nature—the natural rhythms of ocean waves or leaves gently rusting in a summer breeze, of rain falling on the rooftop or a beautiful sunset, of the stars at night or the change of the seasons; each reminds me of this deep connection. When I take time to quiet my body, mind, and spirit and experience natural rhythms, I begin to resonate, to vibrate in-sync, with nature. This promotes a sense of calm and peace and connectedness. I *belong* here.

My "Just for Today" Journal Entry

62.

Just for today...

I accept help from others.

Just for today, I accept help from others. Reiki connects us with others. In 1624, English poet John Donne wrote, "No man is an island entire of itself. Every man is a piece of the continent; a part of the main." Just for today, I reflect upon this gentle reminder. I allow Reiki energy to open my heart and align me with a deep sense of knowing that I am not alone. I am mindful of and receptive to help from others. I willingly share the load of any burden or challenge and gratefully accept assistance. I proactively seek guidance, counsel, and assistance from others.

My "Just for Today" Journal Entry

63.

Just for today...

I acknowledge my own worth.

Just for today, I acknowledge my own worth. I send Reiki to support me in knowing that I am always good enough, always worthy of love, and always whole and complete just as I am in this moment. I acknowledge that "perfect" can be the enemy of "good." When I focus on *how* I am doing rather than on *what* I am doing, I may perceive myself and my efforts as being less than perfect. Reiki supports me in shifting focus away from where I perceive myself to be lacking and towards accepting myself and my efforts through the energy of gentle, loving compassion. Reiki fosters healing, growth, and alignment within me so I may move steadily towards becoming my best self, loving and accepting myself as I am in each moment.

My "Just for Today" Journal Entry

64.

Just for today...

I allow myself to change and grow.

Just for today, I allow myself to change and grow. I intend for the universal life force energy of Reiki to help me move beyond fear, complacency, and resistance to embrace change. I trust Reiki to give me a gentle and loving nudge in the right direction so I may move toward becoming my very best self and fulfilling my highest purpose. I accept and welcome Reiki to connect me with the wisdom, guidance, and loving intent I need most as I experience changes in my body, mind, spirit, and circumstances.

My "Just for Today" Journal Entry

65.

Just for today...

I celebrate my senses.

Just for today, I celebrate my senses. I invite Reiki to align me with a clear experience of the world through the senses gifted to me in this body. I take time to *see* rather than simply look, taking in colors, shapes, light, and shadow. I open my ears to *listen* rather than passively hear, proactively enjoying the voices of my loved ones, my favorite music, and the hum of life all around me. I am grateful for quiet moments and the deep silence from which all sounds arise. I pay attention to taste, celebrating the subtleties of flavor and texture in my food and drink. I breathe in slow and deep, noticing how a simple smell can comfort me, bring me joy, or excite my senses. I touch and take time to truly *feel*. I am grateful that my body allows me to give and receive loving touch. I call upon Reiki with gratitude and the intention of awakening and aligning each of my senses this day towards my highest good.

My "Just for Today" Journal Entry

66.

Just for today...

I honor the value of taking "little steps."

Just for today, I honor the value of taking "little steps." Chinese philosopher Lao Tzu said, "A journey of a thousand miles begins with a single step." I call on Reiki to support me in knowing that taking even a small step towards my goals makes a difference. I commit to taking a small step today, and I send Reiki to my path ahead so I may continue to take small steps each day until I reach my goal. By remaining focused on the small step I am taking right here and now, I am honoring the journey itself and empowering myself to become unstuck. I acknowledge that I am capable of this small step, and I take a step forward.

My "Just for Today" Journal Entry

67.

Just for today...

I remember that I am spirit.

Just for today, I remember that I am spirit. Much in this life encourages us to perceive ourselves as a body having a spiritual experience. Today, I ask Reiki to help me be present to the truth that I am a spiritual being, temporarily housed within this body of flesh and bones. Fat or thin, tall or short, disabled or fully functioning, I am not defined by my body. As a spiritual being, I am the temporary caretaker of the unique configuration of atoms assembled to form this body. The very atoms that comprise my body have previously been part of the food I eat, the water I drink, the air I breathe, even part of countless other human lives before me. My body is not strictly my own; it is a momentary expression of life within the unifying oneness of universal energy. My essence is one with the universal life force. My spirit is timeless and ageless. I send Reiki with the intention that my spirit continues to evolve towards perfect alignment with divine love and light.

My "Just for Today" Journal Entry

68.

Just for today...

I am optimistic and life affirming.

Just for today, I am optimistic and life affirming. I allow myself to appreciate, absorb, and reflect outward all that is good in this life. I send Reiki to my heart with the intention that it may open fully to all life's gifts that are laid out before me. I focus on peaceful, happy feelings, letting any unhelpful emotions roll on by if I encounter them. I acknowledge any physical or emotional pain I feel as a lesson to receive and, ultimately, a gateway to better health and wellness. I choose to be loving and kind. I am grateful for my life. I adopt a "glass-half-full" attitude. I see challenges as opportunities to learn and grow. Just for today, I remember that Reiki is working to unfold everything in my life to be in alignment with my highest health, happiness, and well-being.

My "Just for Today" Journal Entry

69.

Just for today...

I freely and fearlessly express love.

Just for today, I freely and fearlessly express love. I share the energy of loving kindness with everyone I encounter. I say "I love you" to family and friends who are dear to me. I smile and show compassion to strangers I meet throughout my day. I offer hugs freely and let the people in my life know how much they mean to me and how grateful I am for their lives. I make kind gestures, such as buying flowers for my partner or calling a friend whom I haven't spoken with in a while. I am quick to express thanks and slow to anger. Just for today, I choose to operate completely from a place of love.

My "Just for Today" Journal Entry

70.

Just for today...

I remain grounded and fully present in my life.

Just for today, I remain grounded and fully present in my life. I am mindful to maintain awareness of my physical body. I allow myself to be present to the messages it shares with me through aches and pains so I can adjust my eating, physical activity, and water intake to help my body thrive. I send Reiki to any parts of my body that need support. As I walk through my day, I focus my attention on the bottoms of my feet, keeping my awareness grounded with my body and with the earth beneath me. I become present to how nice it feels to be balanced in my human form, filled with spiritual energy that is grounded here in my present existence. I focus on what I am doing rather than how I am doing. I send Reiki with the intention of aligning my personal energy and my life with the peaceful, present, balanced, loving, and grounded energy of love.

My "Just for Today" Journal Entry

71.

Just for today...

I accept all my emotions as valid.

Just for today, I accept all my emotions as valid. I allow myself to feel deeply, honestly, and completely. I let tears fall freely and allow myself full expression of my sorrow or pain. I remember that Reiki is here for me, in good times and bad and I allow Reiki to flow through me and support me in cleansing and clearing any emotions that feel overwhelming. I acknowledge that no one need understand or accept my emotions for them to be valid. Whatever their source, my emotions are coming up to be healed now, and I allow Reiki to flow to all the parts of me—physical, mental, emotional, and spiritual—that need healing. I also allow myself to feel deep joy! I welcome laughter. I choose not to take myself or others too seriously. I honestly acknowledge feelings of anger, fear and other related emotions and call upon Reiki to help me express these feelings appropriately so that I do no harm to myself or others. I remain open, honest, and present, riding my emotions as if riding deep ocean waves. I let each emotion roll over me, feeling it deeply, but not hanging on to it; I let each roll gently away. I feel, I express, and I heal.

My "Just for Today" Journal Entry

72.

Just for today...

I take the time to rest.

Just for today, I take the time to rest. I quiet my body, mind, and spirit. I sit in quiet meditation and allow Reiki energy to fill me with love, light, and peace. I listen to comforting music. I move more slowly and restfully with my physical body. I take an afternoon nap, sunbathe, take a warm bath, read a book, or spend time in nature. I unplug from my digital devices and take time away from phone calls, emails, and social media. I let Reiki nurture, refresh, and revitalize me as I peacefully and gratefully take a day of rest.

My "Just for Today" Journal Entry

73.

Just for today...

I choose to think less and "be" more

Just for today, I choose to think less and "be" more. I allow Reiki to flow through me and help me stay in my heart more than my head. I acknowledge that my brain is a necessary part of my physical vehicle and I choose to put my heart in the driver's seat. I am conscious not to overanalyze people or situations. If these thought patterns arise, I observe them and let them pass on by. I focus on what I am experiencing rather than what I think about it. I become more present to the natural world, listening to the wind and watching it gently move through the leaves. I take a walk around the block and enjoy the sights, sounds, and rhythms of my neighborhood. I allow myself to "just be."

My "Just for Today" Journal Entry

74.

Just for today...

I give myself Reiki.

Just for today, I give myself Reiki. I lay down any "shoulds" or other negative self talk about treating myself every day and know that just for today—each day—is a new opportunity to practice Reiki self-care. I reserve the time and space to allow myself to receive Reiki, whether this is a self-treatment, a session with a local practitioner, or a trade with another Reiki friend. I remember that I can give myself Reiki in the morning as I am waking, on my lunch hour, or at night when I lay down to go to sleep. I make time to receive Reiki healing.

My "Just for Today" Journal Entry

75.

Just for today...

I honor my Reiki family tree.

Just for today, I honor my Reiki family tree. I am grateful for my personal Reiki Master teachers, and for her teachers, and his teachers, and for Hawaya Takata, Chujiro Hayashi, and Mikao Usui, and for the extended line of spiritual seekers and teachers that led to Usui's "discovery" of Reiki. I send Reiki through time and space to bless all my teachers, and their teachers. Just for today, I take time to reflect on the Reiki principles handed down to me. I conduct myself in such a way as to best reflect the love and light my teachers have shared with me. Just for today, my heart is full of gratitude and appreciation for my Reiki lineage.

My "Just for Today" Journal Entry

76.

Just for today...

I share Reiki generously.

Just for today, I share Reiki generously with all who wish to receive it. Mikao Usui freely shared Reiki with thousands. Whenever and wherever he saw pain and suffering, he sent Reiki healing energy. Just for today, I remember that time constraints and distance are not obstacles for Reiki. When I become aware of pain in any living person or thing in my world today, I pause to send Reiki—even if only for a few moments—so that any who wish to receive it may do so. I intend that Reiki bring comfort, peace, and the best possible outcome for the highest good of all whom I encounter.

My "Just for Today" Journal Entry

77.

Just for today...

I am of service to others.

Just for today, I am of service to others. I attend to ways that I may best serve my family, friends, neighbors, and community. I lend a helping hand or donate my time or money to support people and causes that align with loving kindness. I give blood to the Red Cross, read stories to children, or spend time visiting elders in a local nursing home. I ask Reiki to honor my intention of service by providing just the right opportunities where I may be of highest value. I ask that my service be blessed for my highest purpose and that of all whom I serve. I am grateful for the abundance of love and light as it overflows from me to touch the world around me. Just for today, I find my greatest joy in bringing joy to others.

My "Just for Today" Journal Entry

78.

Just for today...

I am inspired.

Just for today, I am inspired. I set the intention that Reiki supports me in welcoming inspiration openly, freely, and fully as I move through this day. I pay attention to the opportunities all around me, allowing my spirit the chance to be inspired to thrive and grow. I look for people, places, and things that move me deeply, spark new ideas, and touch my emotions in ways that encourage me to participate in the activities that nurture my soul. I employ inspiration as a springboard from which to dive deeply into life without reservation towards my highest good and the highest good of all I may impact by way of my newly inspired energy.

My "Just for Today" Journal Entry

79.

Just for today...

I am productive.

Just for today, I am productive. I accomplish that which I set out to accomplish and my efforts are executed with joyful focus and determination. My work is fruitful and I share the harvest of my labors so others may be blessed by my productivity. I send Reiki to support me in working with ease and grace. My productivity comes as the natural outcome of the loving energy I expend. Reiki flows into my work and the product and services created by it. Even as I expend energy, I am filled and revitalized with universal love and light.

My "Just for Today" Journal Entry

80.

Just for today...

I send Reiki to those who have lost a loved one.

Just for today, I send Reiki to those who have lost a loved one. May Reiki give comfort to all who wish to receive it. May those who are grieving ride sorrow and pain as if they are ocean waves that gently move them toward a shore of peace, love, and acceptance. Reiki flows to balance any pain with love, gentleness, sweet memories, and appreciation for the life that has been shared. I allow myself to be a clear channel for Reiki energy, knowing that any who are open to it may feel universal light and love shining into their hearts, connecting them with the source of all love to they know they are never alone. I send Reiki with the intention that death loses its sting as it is framed in its rightful place of the ebb and flow of universal life force energy, which is not bound by time or space. There is no separation , no darkness, no loss within our eternal oneness. Love endures until we are reunited beyond the veil of flesh and bones.

My "Just for Today" Journal Entry

81.

Just for today...

I send Reiki to the worldwide Reiki community.

Just for today, I send Reiki to the worldwide Reiki community. Universal life force energy is present, right here and now, as a unifying field that quickens and connects us. We are truly one body, one community, sparks of love and light that are never separated from the source or from one another. Just for today, I celebrate this oneness and intend that love and light bless our universal Reiki community. I am grateful for this unity and for the deep sense of belonging. I intend that Reiki bless each member of this global community with heightened awareness of our unity. May we know and celebrate each other more fully with each breath.

My "Just for Today" Journal Entry

82.

Just for today...

I send Reiki to my mental health.

Just for today, I send Reiki to my mental health. I am aware of my thoughts as they come and go, and I appreciate that awareness as I observe how my thoughts impact my sense of peace and well-being. I intend that Reiki help me to focus and guide my thoughts toward those that best support my highest good. I let Reiki flow through me to dissolve all negative and harmful thoughts and energies, transmuting them into love and light. I call on Reiki to help me attend to *what* I am doing, not *how* I am doing. Reiki flows to support my mental processes and functions in being healthy, loving, peaceful, and resilient.

My "Just for Today" Journal Entry

83.

Just for today...

I send Reiki to my spiritual health.

Just for today, I send Reiki to my spiritual health. Reiki flows through me, nurturing my spirit and raising the vibration of my personal energies toward ever-increasing alignment with pure love and light. I open myself and invite Reiki to heal any and all of my spiritual wounds, harmful tendencies, bad habits, or addictions, gently and lovingly replacing them with loving kindness, health, and wholeness. May Reiki flow to my spiritual path, supporting me in establishing and maintaining an environment of love and light in which my spirit may thrive and grow. I intend that Reiki bring me only those life experiences and lessons that will enrich my spirit and guide it to optimal health and alignment with love.

My "Just for Today" Journal Entry

84.

Just for today...

I send Reiki to setting healthy boundaries.

Just for today, I send Reiki to setting healthy boundaries. Reiki sends me clear yet gentle reminders that I am worthy of love and life, health and happiness. Reiki's loving guidance helps me to avoid engaging with negative energies that would physically, mentally, or spiritually compromise my well-being. I loving yet unambiguously set and maintain healthy boundaries so my well-being is not compromised by myself or others. I allow myself to be in optimal alignment love, light, and my highest purpose.

My "Just for Today" Journal Entry

85.

Just for today...

I send Reiki to those who have crossed over.

Just for today, I send Reiki to those who have crossed over. May the love and light of Reiki bless and guide those who have moved beyond their physical body and crossed over to a spiritual existence. I allow myself to be a clear channel for Reiki, intending that it flow to remove any fear, disorientation, or trauma and help those who have crossed over move gently and peacefully into alignment with love and light. Reiki flows to dissolve any unhelpful connection that may anchor or burden their spirit from moving beyond this world to fulfill this next part of their spiritual path. May they find love, enlightenment, peace, and joy on their journey.

My "Just for Today" Journal Entry

86.

Just for today...

I send Reiki to artistic expression.

Just for today, I send Reiki to artistic expression. I celebrate the universal life force energy as it manifests in the artistic expressions of the soul. Through music, painting, art, dance, and more, the human spirit communicates with others in life-affirming, creative ways. Just for today, I send Reiki with the intention that my own artistic expression be blessed with love and light, that it may likewise bless me and those with whom I share it. May Reiki bless the energy of the expression itself so that it shines out Reiki to all who encounter it. I allow Reiki to be my guide and my muse. May it eliminate any fear, insecurity, or reluctance toward honestly, fully, and joyfully expressing myself artistically. May it flow to my appreciation and acceptance of others' artistic expressions, free from judgment.

My "Just for Today" Journal Entry

87.

Just for today...

I send Reiki to those who serve.

Just for today, I send Reiki to those who serve. I remember those who have sacrificed themselves in service to others. I send Reiki to veterans, first-responders, and volunteers who place themselves in harms way to defend and protect others. I intend that Reiki heal their wounds of body, mind, and spirit. Reiki blesses them with peace, love, and light. May their service promote their highest good and the highest good of those whom they serve.

My "Just for Today" Journal Entry

88.

Just for today…

I send Reiki to my sleep.

Just for today, I send Reiki to my sleep. Reiki flows to support my healthy sleep patterns so I get just the right amount of sleep for my body and my personal wellness each night. My body, mind, and spirit receive optimal rest as I sleep deeply in complete peace, safety, and comfort. I give myself Reiki as I gently and peacefully drift off to a deep and restful sleep. Reiki blesses my sleep so that it fully refreshes and revitalizes me for the day ahead. When I wake in the morning, I feel aware, alert and rested.

My "Just for Today" Journal Entry

89.

Just for today...

I send Reiki to those who are hungry.

Just for today, I send Reiki to those who are hungry. May Reiki bless them with the food and nourishment they need. I intend that Reiki reveals timely and sustainable strategies to eradicate hunger for our entire global community. May Reiki flow to deepen our awareness and inspire personal, community, and global action and solutions. May Reiki sustain those who hunger, protecting their bodies, minds, and spirits through every moment of lack. May Reiki align human hearts, minds, and actions that we may marshal and manage the abundance of natural and manmade resources available to us so that no one need go hungry.

My "Just for Today" Journal Entry

90.

Just for today...

I send Reiki to the homeless.

Just for today, I send Reiki to the homeless. May Reiki heal and transmute any misaligned personal, community, and environmental energies that have given rise to and maintained the state of homelessness. May all who are homeless be kept safe, protected from the elements, and nourished in body, mind, and spirit. I send Reiki to bring to light a viable and gentle path to sustained shelter in which the homeless may find and maintain a peaceful, healthy, and secure home. May all people be free of suffering and poverty. May Reiki bring all the helpers, resources, and guidance to yield the best possible outcome for the homeless and their highest purpose.

My "Just for Today" Journal Entry

91.

Just for today...

I send Reiki to the unemployed.

Just for today, I send Reiki to the unemployed. I allow Reiki to flow out through me, healing the source of unemployment and blessing the unemployed with new opportunities for work. May Reiki energy be available to all unemployed people who are open to receiving it, guiding them in thought and action toward the optimal new job for their highest purpose. I send Reiki with the intention that they feel encouraged, supported, and peaceful at this time. I ask that Reiki soothe their spirits with calm and sure resolve that "this too shall pass." May Reiki mitigate and transmute any energies that are keeping those who are currently unemployed from realizing joyful abundance. May they know and trust that the right employment outcome will arrive at just the right time for their highest good.

My "Just for Today" Journal Entry

92.

Just for today…

I send Reiki to my intuitive awareness.

Just for today, I send Reiki to my intuitive awareness. I trust my inner knowing and I send Reiki to allow me to better hear my innermost voice, which speaks to this sacred awareness. I remember that we are all born with intuitive abilities that are unique to us, and I ask that Reiki flow to help me become more attuned to my own gifts. Reiki supports me in receiving intuitive messages that are aligned with love and light for my highest good and the highest good all beings. Unhelpful thoughts and confusion dissolve in the light of Reiki so I may receive clear understanding of those messages from spirit and from my higher self that are meant for me.

My "Just for Today" Journal Entry

93.

Just for today...

I move with Reiki.

Just for today, I move with Reiki. Life is in constant motion. With every movement of my muscles, every breath, every step, I move with Reiki flowing through me. As the wind blows, as birds and insects fly by, as people and animals pass me, I bless their movement with Reiki. As the planet turns, as the Moon orbits the Earth, as the planets orbit the Sun, and as our galaxy spins in a universe filled with motion, I send Reiki to bless the beautiful dance of existence.

My "Just for Today" Journal Entry

94.

Just for today…

I send Reiki to my relationships.

Just for today, I send Reiki to my relationships. Reiki works through me to heal those relationships in my life that may not be in alignment with love and light, and I realize that sometimes healing means letting go. Reiki helps me to lovingly remove myself from relationships that are not healthy for me. Reiki supports me in fostering, encouraging, and sustaining relationships that are positive and helpful for me to have in my life. May all my relationships be blessed with healthy boundaries, healthy communication, and the Reiki energy of loving kindness. Reiki blesses each person in the relationship with the physical, mental, and spiritual tools we each need to create optimal outcomes for our highest good.

My "Just for Today" Journal Entry

95.

Just for today...

I become a clearer channel for Reiki.

Just for today, I become a clearer channel for Reiki. With each thought, word, and action that I take today, I intend that Reiki help me to better become a clear channel for universal life force energy. I allow myself to notice that I am more and more able to set my ego aside and allow Reiki to flow through me, unencumbered by my thoughts and feelings. I remember that it is normal and natural to want a certain outcome or hope for things to go a certain way, but I allow myself to observe those desires and then set them down so Reiki can flow through me and work for the highest good of all. I quiet my mind and simply ride the waves of love and light as they are channeled though me. Like a hollow reed, Reiki flows through my body, unobstructed by my ego, my fears, or my desires. Just for today, I remember that becoming a clearer channel begins with my commitment to practice Reiki in my own life as I share Reiki with others.

My "Just for Today" Journal Entry

96.

Just for today...

I send Reiki to a difficult moment in my past.

Just for today, I send Reiki to a difficult moment in my past. Here in this moment, I allow Reiki to guide me to think of an event from my past that hurt me, and from which I am still carrying residual negative energy. As this event comes to mind, I allow Reiki to find the place on my body where I feel a connection to that residual energy and begin to remove the cords and roots of that energy from existence, transmuting them to love and light. Reiki flows through time and space to my past self, allowing me to come through that moment and move forward with my life. Even now, I am receiving new healing benefits from the Reiki that is reaching back in time, helping me to become even more resilient. While I accept this event as part of my growth, I now lay down any negative energies I have been carrying with me since and allow Reiki to heal me completely. I let go, and I heal.

My "Just for Today" Journal Entry

97.

Just for today...

I send Reiki to my next step.

Just for today, I send Reiki to my next step. Remembering that Reiki is already perfectly aligned with light and love and working towards the highest good of all beings, I invite Reiki to help me clear my mind and become open to receiving whatever information I need now. I accept that what I need now may be to wait, and I ask Reiki to guide me in knowing when to have patience and when to take action. Reiki supports me in taking "right action" at the right time—not dwelling in a state of passive inaction, nor "spinning my wheels" and getting in my own way, preventing me from receiving what is best for me. I know and trust that I have all that I need to create my best next step.

My "Just for Today" Journal Entry

98.

Just for today...

I send Reiki to science.

Just for today, I send Reiki to science. I offer huge gratitude from my heart for all of those who, over the millennia, have sought to better understand the working of our physical world in order to help us live more easily within in. I am grateful for the openness of scientists who are willing to test new theories, experiment with new thoughts and technologies, and stretch their minds to encompass both the known and the unknown. I am grateful for those in the scientific community who have incorporated Reiki into their scientific testing. I send Reiki to all those who have helped to make it possible for Reiki healing to reach more people all across the world thanks to scientific study and medical-treatment integration. May science continue to reveal the healing power of Reiki.

My "Just for Today" Journal Entry

99.

Just for today...

I send Reiki to plenty.

Just for today, I send Reiki to plenty. May all beings have plentiful access to food, water, and shelter. I send Reiki to the hearts of those who have plenty, that they may readily share it with those in need. May Reiki flow to heal any place within me that resists residing in a place of plenty. I willingly welcome joyful abundance into my life, knowing that I have all I need to thrive in life, love, work, and spirit!

My "Just for Today" Journal Entry

100.

Just for today...

I remember that it can be easy.

Just for today, I remember that it can be easy. I send Reiki to the parts of myself that carry the energy of resistance, strife, anger, fear, and related emotions. I allow Reiki to gently heal any part of me that, knowingly or unknowingly, is always prepared for a fight or struggle. When I notice myself gearing up for a fight or becoming tense or worried about a situation, I remember the simple truth: It can be easy. Reiki supports me in moving with ease and grace through my life.

My "Just for Today" Journal Entry

101.

Just for today...

I send Reiki to beginnings and endings.

Just for today, I send Reiki to beginnings and endings. I welcome new beginnings into my life with excitement and curiosity, sending Reiki to heal any parts of me that fear change or the unknown. I send Reiki to my ability to acclimate smoothly and easily to new circumstances, learning easily from any mistakes and moving forward with confidence. I remember that with new beginnings come endings. I lovingly let go of the parts of my life that have come to an end so I may fully embrace the new path that is being laid before me. I trust Reiki to help align me with my highest good as I close one door and open another.

My "Just for Today" Journal Entry

Index

abundance 72, 82, 158, 182, 186, 202
air 12, 80, 96, 100, 118, 138
ancestors 54
anger 2, 4, 142, 146, 204
animals 22, 62, 96, 102, 104, 190
art 176
babies 62
bad habit (*see* habits)
bees 104
beginnings 206
birth 34, 62, 112
body 6, 14, 20, 22, 28, 36, 40, 50, 52, 54, 64, 70, 84, 86, 94, 116, 118, 120, 126, 132, 134, 138, 144, 148, 178, 180, 194, 196
boundaries 172, 192
business 3, 80
career 46
cars (*see* vehicles)
challenges 2, 30, 32, 78, 94, 128, 140
change 14, 132, 206
children 58, 158
choices 1, 2, 56, 114
comfort 60, 134, 148, 156, 164, 180
communication 44, 58, 82, 90, 94, 176, 192
community 4, 28, 34, 46, 48, 80, 82, 158, 166, 182, 184, 200
compassion 20, 38, 42, 48, 56, 58, 68, 70, 76, 82, 90, 94, 96, 130, 142
concern 70
conflict 40
confusion 40, 188
country 48, 96
courage 70, 100, 106
creativity 44, 106, 176
dance 176
death 64, 164, 174
dreams 92
drivers 76
earth (*see* land, Mother Earth, planet)
ease 30, 34, 36, 44, 68, 76, 78, 82, 110, 120, 162, 204
ego 26, 56, 78, 114, 194
elders 60, 158
emotions 6, 140, 146, 160, 194, 204
endings 206
environment 122
equality 96
family 10, 46, 68, 96, 142, 154, 158
fathers 108
fear 2, 3, 32, 84, 106, 132, 142, 146, 174, 176, 194, 204, 206
feelings (*see* emotions)
finances 2, 46, 72, 158
first responders 70, 178

Five Reiki Principles 1 – 4
flowers 104, 142
food 10, 12, 20, 22, 52, 102, 134, 138, 182, 202
forgiveness 16, 18, 94
friendship 10, 24, 46, 142, 152, 158
future 3, 24, 30, 34, 82, 86, 116
generosity 3, 156, 158
global warming 124
goals 4, 136
Gokai (*see* Five Reiki Principles)
gratitude 42, 50, 52, 54, 60, 66, 72, 88, 100, 102, 104, 126, 128, 134, 140, 142, 148, 154, 158, 166, 200
grief 164
grounded 52, 100, 144
growth 1, 3, 46, 68, 110, 112, 130, 132, 140, 160, 170, 196
guides 88
habits 90, 98, 170
happiness 1, 2, 3, 4, 30, 46, 102, 140, 172
Hayashi, Chujiro 154
healing 3, 18, 24, 26, 28, 32, 34, 36, 38, 42, 52, 54, 58, 62, 68, 70, 84, 86, 94, 96, 98, 102, 108, 110, 120, 122, 124, 130, 146, 152, 156, 170, 178, 184, 186, 192, 196, 200, 202, 204, 206
health 1, 2, 3, 4, 5, 20, 26, 42, 58, 62, 80, 86, 118, 140, 168, 170, 172, 180
healthcare 42
help 128
home 66
homelessness 184
hunger 182
illness 1, 3, 86, 102, 120
illusion 32, 84, 126
injury 86
insects 52, 190
insecurity 176
inspiration 80, 160, 182
intuition 188
joy 12, 30, 34, 42, 44, 58, 62, 66, 68, 72, 106, 112, 134, 146, 158, 162, 176
kindness 4, 10, 22, 56, 58, 90, 94, 140, 142, 158, 170, 192
land 66, 80, 96, 102
leadership 48, 96
mental health 168
mindfulness 1, 3, 4, 5, 20, 50, 90, 144
money (*see* finances)
Mother Earth 52, 124
mothers 62, 110
music 134, 148, 176
nature 102, 124, 126, 148

neighbors 10, 150, 158
optimism 140
pain 3, 18, 36, 140. 144, 146, 156, 164
parents (*see* fathers, mothers)
past 18, 26, 196
peace 6, 40, 48, 96, 164, 174, 180
planet 34, 50, 52, 100, 102, 104, 116, 118, 122, 124, 190
plants 96, 118
plenty (*see* abundance)
politics (*see* country, leadership)
present 1, 26, 28, 144
productivity 4, 106, 162
purpose 4, 20, 30, 32, 34, 44, 56, 70, 78, 88, 108, 120, 122, 132, 158
race 80
rainforest 122
relationships 3, 94, 192
religion 2, 80
resilience 168, 196
rest 148, 180
right action 198
science 200
self-care 152
self-love 14
self-worth 14, 130, 172
service 42, 158, 178
sleep 152, 180
spiritual guides (*see* guides)
spirituality 64, 88, 138, 170, 174
Takata, Hawaya 154
teachers 82, 154
traveling 74, 76
trees 52, 100, 118, 122
trust 3, 32, 84
truth 90
unemployment 186
Usui, Mikao 1, 3, 5, 154, 156
vehicles 74, 76
war 2, 38, 40
water 20, 50, 80, 96, 116, 138, 144, 202
well-being 30, 72, 140, 168, 172
work 4, 44, 46, 186
worry 2, 3, 30, 32, 72, 204
wounds 26, 86, 102, 170, 178